The Wildflowers of a Berwickshire Bard

(George Henderson of Chirnside, 1800-1864)

Illustrated with plates from

Flora von Deutschland
Österreich und der Schweiz (1885)

Michael E Braithwaite

The Berwickshire Naturalists' Club

2012

ISBN 978-0-9516434-1-9

Printed by Kelso Graphics LLP, Kelso

The Wildflowers of a Berwickshire Bard

The poems of Dr George Henderson, researched and published by his great-great-grandson W G Henderson, reveal him first as a young man commentating passionately on 'The Lowland Clearances' and later as a historian and naturalist with a particular interest in botany recording the massive changes to the countryside that the age of Agricultural Improvers had wrought. This volume celebrates that love of wildflowers. He found most satisfaction in plants that are widespread and truly representative of the countryside of the Borders, only occasionally allowing himself to be distracted by rarities.

Marsh Marigold *Caltha palustris*

Introduction

How well do you relate to wildflowers? Were you brought up to learn their names and to come to appreciate their natural habitats? Not too many of us in Scotland have been so fortunate, even those of us who live in or near the countryside.

I was introduced to botany at an early age and have had a passion for the wildflowers of the Scottish Borders, and Berwickshire in particular, for over forty years. I have found a kindred spirit from the nineteenth century in George Henderson whose poems communicate in a way I cannot match. Henderson not only loved familiar flowers but he also had an instinct for their relation to the plant communities in which they grow. I have chosen extracts from his poems and notebooks to illustrate the different landscape elements of Berwickshire and their wildflowers and have sought to interpret what he writes from my own viewpoint to try to help you share the passion of a botanist.

When you admire a flower in a hedge bank and wish that more were left, do you give a thought to the events two centuries earlier that shaped the land? Henderson lived at Chirnside in Berwickshire at a time when smallholdings, common land and wetland were giving way to large farms with the new steel ploughs and with money for drainage schemes. The path was set that has led to the countryside we know today. Henderson and his family were caught up in the pain of this transition which involved the 'Lowland Clearances'. This compelling drama runs through all that Henderson writes so, as it affected the wildflowers just as harshly as the people on the land, I have let the 'Clearances' become the second theme of this book to lend perspective when you view the fragmented wildlife habitats that remain today.

Michael Braithwaite
August 2012

Contents

Billie Mire looking west

The Literary Sources

The extracts of Dr George Henderson's works quoted in this book are drawn from three sources. The first is his collected poems published by his great-great-grandson W G Henderson as *Merse Local Rhymes and Other Poems* 2009, the second is George Muirhead's two-volume *The Birds of Berwickshire* 1889, 1895 and the third is Henderson's unpublished notebooks.

Merse Local Rhymes and Other Poems is in two sections. One is a facsimile of Henderson's *The Scenes of Boyhood; and other poems* published in 1840, though written somewhat earlier, the other presents for the first time in book form his poems from the 1850's, most of which were originally published in the pages of the *Berwick Advertiser*.

Henderson compiled extensive notebooks with a view to publishing *The Merse Dictionary*, an account of the history and antiquities of the district. While he never completed this project, a large part of his notes, but not the botany, was published posthumously by the Berwickshire Naturalists' Club in 1900 as *The Historical and Descriptive Account of Buncle and Preston* and a manuscript copy was made by John Blair for George Muirhead, factor of the Paxton estates, who utilised extracts of the prose and poetry in his lavish two-volume work *The Birds of Berwickshire* 1889, 1895. These manuscript notebooks survive and are held at the Heritage Hub in Hawick.

Although *Flora von Deutschland Österreich und der Schweiz* 1885, the source of most of the illustrations in this book, is a later work and might have been beyond Henderson's budget, he would have appreciated it as it shares the artistry and attention to detail that is a hallmark of his writings. John Blair's illustrations in Muirhead's *The Birds of Berwickshire* have also been drawn on.

The Life of Dr George Henderson

George Henderson was born in 1800 in the old farmhouse of Little Billy (or Billie), in the parish of Bunkle, near Chirnside in Berwickshire. Thereabouts were a group of small farmers, tenants of the great estate of the Homes of Wedderburn Castle and Paxton House. All were dispossessed when George was twelve so that the farm of Billie Mains could be enlarged and improved. A great wetland at Billie Mire was drained, the moor above enclosed and ploughed and the fields restructured in a more regular pattern to permit effective use of the new swing-plough.

John Henderson, George's father, was very fortunate. The Homes granted him another tenancy, this time for 21 years, on the small farm of Greenhead, just a few miles away near the village of Auchencrow. George was fortunate too, as the school master at Auchencrow was John Strauchan, a Greek and Latin scholar of high repute. George took full advantage of a much more rigorous schooling than could have been expected to come his way and entered Edinburgh University when he was nineteen to study English. It did not work out, though his love of poetry probably developed at this period, and it was not until he was twenty-five that he returned to Edinburgh to study medicine at the Royal College of Surgeons where he was duly licensed in 1829. He set up in business at Chirnside and stayed there the rest of his days. He was doctor to ordinary folk and, while his practice was not a prosperous one, he was much loved in his district. An early sweetheart died and he did not marry till he was thirty-seven when he met a local girl of seventeen. The marriage was a success, though marred by the loss of his first child and other tragedies.

Henderson was a founder member of the Berwickshire Naturalists' Club, formed in 1831 by Dr George Johnston of Berwick-upon-Tweed. It brought together a very lively group of young men, mainly fellow medics and ministers who had trained together in

Edinburgh. Johnston was one of the fellow medics, though a much more prosperous one. Henderson could not spare the time to attend the Club's meetings, so he dropped out quite soon but kept up his contact by correspondence. His writings are strongly influenced by the example of its members, particularly Johnston, Alexander Carr and James Hardy. Poetry was one of Johnston's many interests and there is evidence of a strong mutual respect between the two men. Astonishingly, Henderson had built up a library of over 2,250 books by the time of his death and its sale catalogue, which survives, contains items suggesting that part of it may have come to Henderson on Johnston's death.

Although many poets have used wildflowers in their imagery, few have had more than a general countryman's knowledge. George Henderson is an exception, as his prose writings make it clear that he had a detailed knowledge of the species present in Berwickshire, in rather the way that the poet John Clare had in Northamptonshire.

There is a contrast between the impassioned rustic style of youth in *The Scenes of Boyhood* and the mellow writings of a well-read man in later years. Henderson records that he liked reciting poetry during his long hours on horseback attending to his country practice and one can infer that he rehearsed his own poetry likewise. Many of the poems that survive were written in later life and in them Henderson reworks again and again images developed in his early poetry and in his notebooks, perhaps partly because by then he had so little time for the leisured wanderings in the countryside which might have given him further inspiration.

George Henderson was a great observer of people and nature and that did not change over the years, nor did he lose his practical concern and sense of injustice for the hardship suffered by man and nature during the great changes wrought by the industrial and agricultural revolution of his times. Tragedy was a fact of life in Henderson's times and he experienced a full share of it.

The Lowland Clearances

Henderson's early literary interests were much influenced by John Leyden of Denholm, Roxburghshire. His *Scenes of Boyhood* are clearly modelled on Leyden's *Scenes of Infancy*, a saga of a hundred and forty pages published in 1803. There is one passage in particular which must have struck a very personal chord and which Henderson copied into his notebooks. It is reproduced here as an introduction to Henderson's poems on the 'Lowland Clearances'. The bitterness felt by the country people at the changes that had overwhelmed them and left them to suffer great hardship is captured by Leyden and Henderson, both of whom experienced it all 'at the sharp end'.

So what were these changes? The Union of Crowns in 1603 ended centuries of Border warfare promising more settled times in which agriculture could develop, but there were interruptions from the Civil War in 1642 and the Rebellion of 1745 so progress was slow until the second half of the eighteenth century.

Henderson describes the part then played by Dr James Hutton: 'His father, who was a respectable merchant in Edinburgh, having left him the farm of Slighhouses [almost adjacent to Billie Mains], he turned his attention to agriculture, and for some time resided in the county of Norfolk, for the purpose of studying the modes of husbandry practised there; and travelling through Holland, Brabant, Flanders, and Picardy for the same end. He returned to Scotland about the middle of summer 1754, and shortly after commenced improvements on his patrimonial estate. From Norfolk he brought with him a plough [the Suffolk swing-plough] and ploughmen, and here exhibited the first example of good tillage. It was a novel sight for the surrounding farmers to see the plough drawn by two horses, without an accompanying driver, instead of the rude clumsy ploughs dragged along by four horses, or four or six owsen [oxen], and driven by a gauds-man. The new system was, however, found to succeed in all its parts, and was in a few years adopted by the principal farmers of Berwickshire'.

A little later James Small returned from the south and in 1763 developed a much improved version of the swing-plough at a forge specially built for him at Blackadder Mount, just across the river from Chirnside. Small's Plough was an immediate success and, coupled with improved crop varieties, proved to be the spur to action. Meanwhile the large estates were employing land surveyors who drew up long-term plans for improvements. Then the Napoleonic wars of 1793-1815 caused a jump in commodity prices. There was a boom period in agriculture with a rush to develop with all speed and at any cost; little wonder when improvements could lead to a doubling in rents and the price increases to a doubling again.

Small's Swing-plough

Some landlords were caught out after the war when prices fell back and some of the poorer land proved uneconomic to cultivate and was returned to rough sheep grazing. This sometimes delayed steps to improve the lot of the farm hinds and part-time workers.

But the countryside had been changed forever in just a few decades. The patchwork of historic farmsteads with in-bye fields and out-bye pasturage on open unenclosed moorland, with little in the way of woodland, was replaced by a planned landscape of large farms with enclosed fields divided to suit the crop rotation of the day, with new farmhouses and steadings and with new plantations, mainly for shelter rather than timber. Amid this the large estates grew prosperous indeed and the great houses of the Borders were enlarged or rebuilt and their policies were laid out in the grand manner.

It was not all loss for those displaced from the land. The textile industry prospered and there were opportunities in the army and navy and in the colonies overseas. But the social structures on the land were changed forever.

The Suffolk poet Robert Bloomfield wrote in 1798 of the Suffolk swing-plough (the forerunner of Small's):

> No wheels support the diving pointed share
> No groaning ox is doomed to labour there,
> No helpmates teach the docile steed his road,
> Alike unknown the ploughboy and his goad,
> But, unassisted through each toilsome day,
> With smiling brow the ploughman cleaves his way.

Oxen ploughing

John Leyden's
Scenes of Infancy: descriptive of Teviotdale
published 1803

I recognise Leyden as a true countryman who weaves plants into his tale as he tells of the injustice done to the smallholders of Roxburghshire. Elsewhere in his saga he paints a more detailed picture of the countryside of Teviotdale with birds and bees set in their places, as well as flowers, ferns and trees. The habitat losses that came with the agricultural improvements had not become critical in Teviotdale as early as 1803, so Leyden does not have reason to dwell on them. That, as we shall see, was left to Henderson.

The following passage on the 'Lowland Clearances' was that copied out by Henderson:

No more the cottage roof, fern-thatched and gray,
Invites the weary traveller from the way,
To rest, and taste the peasant's simple cheer,
Repaid by news and tales he loved to hear;
The clay-built wall, with woodbine[1] twisted o'er,
The house-leek[2], clustering green above the door,
While, through the sheltering elms, that round them grew,
The winding smoke arose in columns blue;—
These all have fled; and, from their hamlets brown,
The swains have gone, to sicken in the town,
To pine in crowded streets, or ply the loom;
For splendid halls deny the cottage room.
Yet on the neighbouring heights they oft convene,
With fond regret to view each former scene,
The level meads, where infants wont to play

---

[1] Honeysuckle *Lonicera periclymenum*
[2] A stonecrop *Sempervivum tectorum*, once popular on farmhouse roofs and walls in the belief that it could ward off lightning, but now very seldom seen

Around their mothers, as they piled the hay,
The hawthorn hedge-row, and the hanging wood,
Beneath whose boughs their humble cottage stood.
   Gone are the peasants from the humble shed,
And with them too the humble virtues fled:
No more the farmer, on these fertile plains,
Is held the father of the meaner swains,
Partakes, as he directs, the reaper's toil,
Or with his shining share[1] divides the soil,
Or in his hall, when winter nights are long,
Joins in the burthen of the damsel's song,
Repeats the tales of old heroic times,
While BRUCE and WALLACE consecrate the rhymes.
These all are fled—and, in the farmer's place,
Of prouder look, advance a dubious race,
That ape the pride of rank, with aukward state,
The vice, but not the polish, of the great,
Flaunt, like the poppy[2], mid the ripening grain,
A nauseous weed, that poisons all the plain.
The peasant, once a friend, a friend no more,
Cringes, a slave, before the master's door;
Or else, too proud, where once he loved, to fawn,
For distant climes deserts his native lawn,
And fondly hopes, beyond the western main
To find the virtues, here beloved in vain.

---

[1] The new steel plough

[2] Today we think of the wild poppies *Papaver dubium* and *P. rhoeas* as threatened species and forget their very real nuisance to the farmer before the days of herbicides

House-leek *Sempervivum tectorum*

George Henderson's *Scenes of Boyhood*
published 1840

As noted above this poem was modelled on Leyden. Henderson introduces it with a long preamble. 'Part of my object in the following Poem was to show the evils and injustice of Monopolies in Agriculture..... Let landlords consider what misery they create to thousands, by dispersing their small tenantry, and throwing down their ancient dwellings..... You will perhaps object that I have been needlessly severe on the wealthy and titled classes of society. ..... But far be from me, the uncharitableness to include *all* in these sweeping charges and denunciations; there are glorious, noble, magnanimous exceptions.....'

> Now Fancy turn, to yon old hoary trees,
> That stand, a lonely group, shook by the autumnal breeze;
> There stood our cottage 'neath the flickering shade,
> Skirted by garden snug in rose and mint arrayed;
> In sunny nook the hives in order stood,
> With busy inmates storing up their food;
> The raspberry[1] there, and currants flourish'd sweet,
> And gooseberry too – for boys a famous treat!
> Byre, shed and barn, behind the ha' were plac'd,
> And many a grassy plot the sheltered hamlet grac'd,
> Where thrifty goodwife bleach'd her linens white,
> And boys and girls there, like fairies light;
> A row of thatch'd cots stood by the croft-land green,
> Where lads and lasses by the doors were seen,
> When gloamin grey bedimm'd the distant vale,
> Listening to rustic song, or fairy tale;
> While the loud laugh rung through the merry band,
> And the wild harping craik[1], called from the clover land:

---

[1] Raspberry *Rubus idaeus* is found not only in its cultivated form but as a wild plant

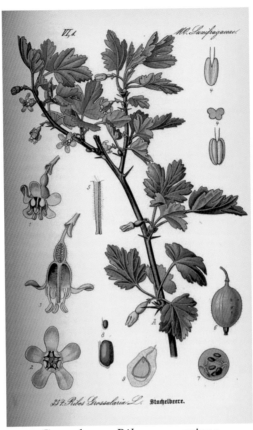

Gooseberry *Ribes uva-crispa*

But darker night came o'er the ridgy lea,
And chill the breeze sighed through the aged tree:
Then 'round the hearth the cottagers withdrew,
And hoary sires gave all monitions due;
And now the Holy Book is from the crevice ta'en,
And praise and prayer, in simple fervent strain,
Is uttered forth beside the cottage fire,
By man and maiden, matron, child and sire;
When worship's o'er and supper at an end,

---

[1] Corncrake

16

All to their rest the rustic inmates bend;
And there in sweet repose their wearied bodies lie,
Till the lark calls them up their daily tasks to ply.

But there no more the evening psalm we'll hear,
Nor song nor glee shall the soft breezes bear:-
The green is gone – the garden bower's away,
And all our homestead levelled with the clay:
No more our feet will tread the cottage green,
Nor there again will cot or ha' be seen;
Still stand the trees, like ancient veterans there,
And wild the blast moans through the branches bare;
But there no more shall be what once hath been;
For fell Monopl'y triumphs o'er the scene;
And bloated grows, like hemlock[1] by the wall,
The monster vile, that makes our country fall!

---

[1] Hemlock *Conium maculatum* was a valued, but dangerous, medicinal plant, that has a remarkable ability to survive on the ruins, if the buildings where it has been cultivated should fall. It has curious swollen, red-spotted stems that seem to herald a plant of ill-repute. Nowadays it is altogether more frequent in the east of Berwickshire especially on steep banks above the Tweed, but in the west, and in Roxburghshire, it is less common. I have observed it with some surprise on the ruins of Overton Tower, at 250m above Camptown near Jedburgh, and it grows by an old byre at our own home at Clarilaw, which much predates the Victorian farmhouse

Hemlock *Conium maculatum*

But Henderson, to a far greater extent than Leyden, and perhaps rivalled only by John Clare in Northamptonshire, sees the changes not just as the end of a way of life for the 'cottars' but as a disaster for the natural world:

> I love the uncultured spot, where Nature revels free,
> Some place left sacred to the flower and bee –
> But few such spots now near our home remain,
> All must be torn, to add unto our gain:
> The marsh and *common* now must feel the share,
> And culture's hand be busy everywhere:
> Our land does flourish, say the great and wise –
> Improvement's march makes still the markets rise;
> The rich men richer grow, and roll about at ease;
> And bloated luxury doth her fancy please;

Henderson soon turns to his own particular loss, Billie Mire:

> Where countless reeds once clothed yon narrow vale,
> Their feathery heads wild streaming in the gale –
> There lay the Myre, with moss-pools dark and deep,
> The wild grey willows waving there you'd see,
> Their silvery blossoms opening to the bee;
> There red marsh cinque-foil and the buck-bean[1] grew,
> And hoary cannach[2] waving in the view;
> The yellow marigold[3] long flourished there,
> And purple orchis[4] – Flora's offerings fair:
> The pale-flower'd cresses[5] o'er the water spread,
> And broad green flags[6] with graceful drooping head:

Marsh Cinquefoil *Potentilla palustris*

---

[1] Marsh Cinquefoil *Potentilla palustris* and Bogbean *Menyanthes trifoliata*, two plants of moderately acid fen

[2] A Gaelic word for Common Cottongrass *Eriophorum angustifolium*, another fen specialist

[3] Marsh Marigold *Caltha palustris*

[4] Here in the mire Northern Marsh-orchid *Dactylorhiza purpurella*

[5] Water-cress *Rorippa nasturtium-aquaticum agg.*

[6] Yellow Iris *Iris pseudacorus* with its large green fruit-pods

Or, seen from the viewpoint of his own childhood:

> Nor less remember'd is the path remote,
> Which to the school we travers'd to our cot;
> Oft careless, there we loitered by the way,
> To pluck the flowers, or chase the insects gay;
> 'Midst the wild bracken, and the meadow's queen[1],
> We've ranged the dell – a truant band unseen;
> Or 'mong the whins, with yellow blossoms drest,
> We sought the lintwhite's[2] and the yorlin's[3] nest;
> Or climb'd the braes the liquorice knots[4] to dig;
> Or chas'd the peesweep[5] o'er the braided rig[6],
> Or scal'd the trees to harry rooks and daws[7]
> Or roam'd the dean to gather hips and haws;
> Or by yon banks we lingered night and morn,
> To hook the minnows from the wimpling[8] burn;

When I walk through Berwickshire's countryside on my botanizing rambles in the spring and summer, it often strikes me as remarkable how few people I meet there. I enjoy a few words with the occasional shepherd or keeper and there are fishermen, but other walkers keep to way-marked footpaths and children are nowhere to be seen, except on the main beaches at the coast. There is no 'truant band', except close to caravan parks where an occasional rope may be slung as a swing from an overhanging bough. The farmers must be grateful for this, but there are now whole generations who have missed out on an experience of 'the wild'.

---

[1] Meadowsweet *Filipendula ulmaria*
[2] Linnet
[3] Yellow-hammer
[4] Bitter-vetch *Lathyrus linifolius*, which has tuberous roots
[5] Lapwing
[6] Cultivated strip of land
[7] Jackdaws
[8] meandering

Dog-rose *Rosa canina agg.*

Hawthorn *Crataegus spp.*

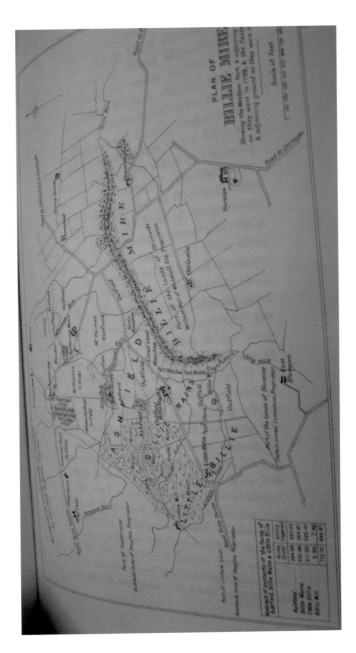

Map of Billie Mire

22

Childhood by Billy Myre (Billie Mire)

To my mind there is something very special about Henderson's account of his childhood by Billie Mire. Only in the poems of John Clare in Northamptonshire have I met such a vivid portrayal at this early date of the loss of wildlife at a particular place and its impact on those who lived beside it. Henderson tells the tale both in prose and verse though neither was written in childhood. They were written after Henderson had studied in Edinburgh and had qualified as a surgeon, relearning his botany more formally and being exposed to the writings and poetry of his day.

It takes little imagination to generalise in one's mind from the particular to what was happening in Berwickshire as a whole and indeed all over lowland Scotland. This was indeed the time when so many wetlands were drained with little sense of a need to balance the needs of agriculture with those of wildlife. Equally far-reaching were the effects of the ploughing of moor and rough pasture and small-scale drainage at the burnsides. Many of the wildflowers survived these changes on knowes and in awkward corners which were not worth the effort of improvement. In my own lifetime it has been these last refuges that have been steadily destroyed, by fertilising, by drainage mechanised with JCBs and by lack of grazing until the poor remnants have been judged to be of too little value and have been converted to the ponds and small woodlands championed by conservationists[1].

In taking the following paragraphs from Henderson's notebooks I have updated the botanical Latin names:

'The long narrow valley called Billy Myre formed in former times a deep morass – stretching from east to west about five miles in length.

---

[1] The illustration on the front cover shows a burnside fragment with ancient alders and Pignut *Conopodium majus* that has survived at Billie Castle to 2012

It forms the boundary between the parishes of Coldingham and Chirnside. A few years ago it was thickly covered with Common Bog Reed[1] *Phragmites australis*, several species of large sedge *Carex*, Marsh Marigold *Caltha palustris*, Wild Angelica *Angelica sylvestris*, Marsh Cinquefoil *Potentilla palustris*, Hemlock Water-dropwort *Oenanthe crocata*, Bogbean *Menyanthes trifoliata*, Fool's Water-cress *Apium nodiflorum*[2], Marsh Violet *Viola palustris*, Brooklime *Veronica beccabunga*, Water-cress *Rorippa nasturtium-aquaticum agg.*, Cuckoo-flower *Cardamine pratensis*, several species of Cotton-grass *Eriophorum*, *Scirpus*[3], Willows *Salix*, Yellow Iris *Iris pseudacorus*, Bulrush *Typha latifolia*, several species of Rush *Juncus*, Pondweeds *Potamogeton*, Marsh Ragwort *Senecio aquaticus*, Water Forget-me-not *Myosotis scorpioides* and many other marsh plants[4]. Before this Myre was drained there was also found in it, in considerable abundance, the Medicinal Leech *Hirudo medicinalis*. Specimens of the most of the plants in the above list may still be procured here, although their abundance has been sadly thinned by the progress of cultivation.

Billy Myre has been drained by a ten or twelve foot ditch more than twenty years ago carried along its whole length from east to west, and by smaller drains running into this, and what was formerly an impassable quagmire now bears most exuberant crops of grain, especially of oats.

Before it was drained Billy Myre was the resort of numerous wildfowl, especially ducks which used to visit it in thousands. Very few of these birds are now seen in the neighbourhood.

---

[1] Common Reed

[2] This may have been Lesser Water-parsnip *Berula erecta*

[3] Probably Common Club-rush *Schoenoplectus lacustris*

[4] Tiny fragments of this mire survive, cut off from the Billie Burn by the embankment of the old railway

Bogbean *Menyanthes trifoliata*

Blaeberry *Vaccinium myrtillus*

On the bank of a stream between Lintlaw and Billy Mains, a number of tall grey ash trees of venerable appearance are seen standing in solitary grandeur in a field near the wayside. These trees surrounded the old farmhouse and onstead of Little Billy, which have long since been levelled with the dust. On the banks of this stream several interesting plants are to be found, the Wood Anemone or Windflower *Anemone nemorosa*, Ground-ivy *Glechoma hederacea*, Earth nut or Arnut[1] *Conopodium majus*. We have often in our juvenile days dug up the bulbous roots of this plant and regaled ourselves upon them both boiled and raw. We are persuaded that they would make a very useful article of food, but children are often deterred from eating them from an idea that they make people lousy. On the bank of the burn on the west we have an abundance of Blaeberry *Vaccinium*

---

[1] Pignut

myrtillus, Hard Fern *Blechnum spicant*, with mosses and liverworts. In the stream itself grows the Branched Bur-reed *Sparganium erectum*, Yellow Iris *Iris pseudacorus*, and the Fool's Water-cress *Apium nodiflorum[1]*. The margin of the stream is bordered in many places with the pleasing Meadowsweet *Filipendula ulmaria*, and two varieties of Mint *Mentha*. Above Billy Mill (now no more, as it was taken down in December 1845) in a meadow now planted the Globe-flower *Trollius europaeus* grows in profusion with the Water Avens *Geum rivale*, which latter plant grows in this station with greater luxuriance than we have ever seen elsewhere. In a lane which runs between the lands of Little Billy and Lintlaw we found several patches of the Northern Bedstraw *Galium boreale*.'

Water Avens *Geum rivale*

---

[1] This may have been Lesser Water-parsnip *Berula erecta*

Song[1], December 14, 1832

By Billy burn in the lang syne days,
    The globe-flower[2] oft I have plucked with thee,
Or wandered about on the mossy braes
    Chasing the dragon fly and wild red bee –

But by bog or burn thou wilt no more be
    To cast thy smile on my weary way;
And O! at our kirn[3] there's been little glee
    Since thou wert laid i' the silent clay.

'In the woods about Blackburn near the eastern extremity of Billy Myre several fine plants will be found to reward the research of the Botanist and in the neighbouring marshy ground to the north of Edington Hill, the Marsh Orchis *Dactylorhiza purpurella*, Spotted Orchis *Dactylorhiza maculata* or *D. fuchsii* and Aromatic Orchis [4] *Gymnadenia conopsea* grows abundantly. At Blackburn we have also noticed very tall (at least nine feet in height) specimens of Common Broom *Cytisus scoparius*'.

---

[1] Written in memory of his tragically deceased sister Helen
[2] The *Trollius europaeus* – the Luckan gowan of Allan Ramsay [Henderson's footnote]
[3] In the sense of a harvest thanksgiving feast
[4] Fragrant Orchid

Marsh-orchid *Dactylorhiza sp.*

Jock o' the Myre, May 31, 1855
Billie Mire was held to be the haunt of a fearful ghost. I have little doubt that this was a tale based on the booming cry of the bittern which used to breed there in the reed beds. Henderson may never have heard the bittern, which had been shot almost to local extinction before the mire was fully drained. In his poem Henderson vividly depicts the habitat using the local vernacular of his childhood.

In yon deep morass, low under the knowe,
The paddocks[1] were croupin'[2] down i' the howe[3];
In the black peat holes, a' slimy and caller[4],
The filthy asks[5] and taeds[6] did waller;
And the grey saugh-bushes[7] were dimly seen,
Wi' reeds, and seggs[8], and humlocks[9] green
When Jock o' the Myre, at midnight hour,
Through the wreaths o' mist did gape and glower.

Wild Angelica *Angelica sylvestris*

---

[1] frogs
[2] croaking
[3] hollow
[4] cool
[5] newts
[6] toads
[7] willows
[8] sedges
[9] Large umbellifers (rather than hummocks), here likely to be Wild Angelica *Angelica sylvestris*

30

Childhood, July 16, 1856

This is a wide-ranging poem of childhood days, with the wildflowers a recurring theme. Henderson captures just the sort of habitat combination that has suffered most: a burn with its margins undrained and knowes with unimproved grassland.

> Where blue curly-doddies[1] bloom bright on the knowes,
> And the burn through the flags[2], in its loneliness rowes[3],
> O there – never will your haunts be again
> But toss'd unreposing on life's stormy main.

Field Scabious *Knautia arvensis*

---

[1] Here in The Merse Field Scabious *Knautia arvensis*, which grows on dry banks and knowes, but in the Lammermuirs another Scabious of wet places, Devil's-bit Scabious *Succisa pratensis*, and in England Ribwort Plantain *Plantago lancelota*. Various games were played with such flowers: the flower on a good long stalk could be used like conkers (but without the string) to try to knock the head off an opponent's flower, or the stalk could be held upside-down and the head twisted and then released to spin like a top The name may come from Jacobite days and be corrupted diminutives of Charles and George who were truly trying to knock the other's head off to become undisputed king

[2] Yellow Iris *Iris pseudacorus*

[3] rolls

We'll meet nae mair by Draedan Burn, August, 1855

A lament at the draining and ploughing of Billie Mire and the adjacent meadows by the Draedan Burn with the displacement of the smallholders, 'cottars', who had lived there.

> Nae mair we'll meet by Draedan burn,
> Wi' maidens blythe[1] as e'er were born,
> To tedd[2] the hay, or lint[3] to steep[4]
> Down in the moss-holes dark and deep;
> The holes are drain'd – the saugh-buss grey[5],
> The bog-reeds[6] tall in plum'd array,
> And red moss flowers[7], are a' uptorn –
> Nae mair we'll meet by Draedan burn.

---

[1] joyful

[2] spread out to dry

[3] Flax *Linum usitatissimum*

[4] soak, to soften the fibres before retting

[5] Willows

[6] Common Reed *Phragmites australis*

[7] Similar words used elsewhere by Henderson point to this being Marsh Cinquefoil *Potentilla palustris*

Billie Mire

A Lament to the Bog Reeds, September 4, 1855
The reed beds formed the largest habitat in Billie Mire. The main ditch through the mire had been dug in 1801 or 1802, just after Henderson was born, with further draining and ploughing only proceeding in stages over a period of many years.

> But mostly, I lament the loss
> O' tall bog-reeds[1] that leaned across
> The black moss-pits and glitty foss[2] –
> And bog-reeds slim[3],
> That wav'd their plumes o' purple gloss
> O'er well-heads dim.

---

[1] Two kinds of bog-reed are implied, the tall stout one is likely to be Bulrush *Typha latifolia* which was a feature of the mire
[2] slimy ditch
[3] Common Reed *Phragmites australis* which has purple flowers

A further fragment given by Muirhead to illustrate his account of the Reed Bunting refers specifically to the Bulrush, but I have not traced the whereabouts of Kelpie's Hole: it may have been just a small area of open water within Billie Mire.

> Where meadow-blooms, red, drooping hang[1],
> O'er stream and pool, and bog reeds lang
> Wave slowly, and bull-rushes strang
>   Shade Kelpie's Hole[2].

Bulrush *Typha latifolia*

---

[1] Similar words used elsewhere by Henderson point to this as being Great Willowherb *Epilobium hirsutum*

[2] A kelpie is a water spirit

Muirhead uses Henderson again in his account of the Corncrake. Piper's knowe was at the east end of Billie Mire and was said to have been a favourite haunt of the fairies.

> On the Pyper's knowes, where the lang broom grows,
> I sat me down in the gloamin' dim;
> While lay the white mist on the reedy Mire's breast,
> And the Crake 'mang the corn sang his evening hymn.

Nature's lament for Man's encroachments, c.1840?
Henderson takes up the themes of his *Scenes of Boyhood* with the more measured words of maturity, but still with the same deep-seated conviction of tragedy.

> Our bonny burn-sides they hae drained and dug,
>> The crook o' the burn they have altered too;
> The green ferny knowes, where the hare lay snug,
>> They hae cleared o' ilka buss, and riven wi' the pleugh,
> The bonny green braes by the foggy dell,
>> Where grew the broom and the black slae-thorn[1],
> They hae levelled down with a purpose fell,
>> And Nature laments a' her beauties torn.

From my perspective as a botanist there has been no let up in 'man's encroachments' to this day. It is true that attitudes have changed remarkably in the last twenty years with much activity in the name of wildlife conservation, but the focus has been very largely on farm woodlands, hedges, new ponds and the fencing-off of riversides. The result is an obsessively tidy countryside that the farmer feels proud of. But there have been losses along the way, as Henderson saw so clearly, to the unfertilized grassland on the knowes, to the scrubby banks, to the wet hollows and to the cattle-plodged riversides. All of

---

[1] Sloe or Blackthorn *Prunus spinosa*

these are key habitats for wildflowers and invertebrates. There is more breeding cover for birds, but less insect food, so expensive setaside strips and special crops are provided for bird-seed and game cover to try to redress the balance. I wonder whether this is an efficient use of resources and lament the 'wild places' slipping away.

Sloe or Blackthorn *Prunus spinosa*

Schooldays at Auchencrow

Henderson's recalls his schooldays (1812-1818) at Auchencrow as follows (the botanical names are updated):

'On the southeast skirts of Dreedreigh hill lie the farms of Shillunderlies and Swansfield. At the foot on the south is situated the ancient village of Auchencrow. It is a small dull sequestered place, straggling along the southern bank of a small stream about seven miles to the east of Dunse. It supports a school in which is taught the common branches of education. Here Mr John Strauchan, present schoolmaster of Swinton, taught a large school for several years. Mr Srauchan is well known as an excellent Greek scholar, both at home and abroad, and the present professor of Greek in the University of Edinburgh was educated under him. This village is also noted as the birthplace of James Bonnar, author of a work on Bees, and the inhabitants of this place seem to have inherited from him a predilection for this branch of rural economy – Mr George Burns, weaver here, being one of the greatest bee masters in the country.

We have many pleasant recollections connected with Auchencrow, of its old thatched and straggling houses, interspersed by 'kail yards green' with their frail fences of grey stones and bourtree bushes – of its burn skirting the village on the north side in which were found plenty of stickleback, loaches, eels and minnows, and above all of its old women who were reckoned the fellest of witches. The schoolhouse then stood on a gently sloping bank at the east end of the village, but removed to a small distance from the line of the street and on the north side of the brook. It was called 'Grammar Hall' and it long bore that title over its door, painted on a piece of board. It is now a joiner's shop and its windows are closed up. I never pass it without looking with many painfully pleasing regrets and associations, on its humble thatched roof – and on the row of 'bourtrees' which skirts the roadside in front of the lovely mansion.

These bourtrees had a very inviting look in Autumn when thickly clustered with their purple berries, of which our preceptor's wife was wont to manufacture her Elderberry wine. A little to the southeast lies our playground – a small green by the pathway side leading to Chirnside, and a green farther up nearer the village which has been appropriated by some greedy laird afflicted with that most pestilential disease 'the yird hunger'. Here we have often joined in the games of football, shinty, Scottish and English hatty, marbles &c with companions who are all scattered abroad: some in prosperity, some in adversity and toiling for their daily bread, many bowed down with care and sorrow and many of them now sleeping in the lone churchyard. What fond illusions swarm by that burnside which quietly flows away to the green meadows on the east. Often have we paidled in that burn! Often have we caught minnows in that brook! Often have we slaked our thirst at the clear and copious fountain which issues from the fence on the north margin of the stream a little to the east of the green above mentioned – the beautiful Meadow Well. These scenes seem now dwindled into insignificance and appear desolate and forlorn, possibly because we have outlived our boyish innocence and glee; but still possess for me an indescribable charm which can only pass away with life itself.

Auchencrow Village

Oxeye Daisy *Leucanthemum vulgare*

In the meadow to the E. of Auchencrow once grew the Bulrush *Typha latifolia*. It will now be sought for there in vain. About a mile to the east of the village in a ditch between Moormountrigg and Stoneshiel Dr Robert Hood found the Water Purslane *Lythrum portula* (the Water Poplin of Allan Ramsay) and in the same ditch we found the charming Grass-of-Parnassus *Parnassia palustris* flourishing in all its beauty, and on the adjoining moor there is abundance of Oxeye Daisy *Leucanthemum vulgare*, Creeping Cinquefoil *Potentilla reptans*, Butterwort *Pinguicula vulgaris*, Eyebright *Euphrasia officinalis*, Common Yellow Rattle *Rhinanthus minor*, and on the neighbouring farm of Greenhead will be found rather abundantly the Red Bartsia *Odontites vernus*, Selfheal *Prunella vulgaris* and on the same farm sparingly the Pepper-saxifrage *Silaum silaus*'.

The village itself has not changed all that much over the years, but the same is not true of the burn. I guess that its minnows will be looked for in vain and I believe that many of its wildflowers are gone. Watercress *Nasturtium microphyllum* remains but, outside the cultivated fields, the margins are overshadowed by Great Willowherb *Epilobium hirsutum*, Russian Comfrey *Symphytum x uplandicum* and coarse grasses, festooned in places by Hedge Bindweed *Calystegia sepium* all of which have spread greatly since Henderson's day in response to the increased use of fertilisers.

Butterwort *Pinguicula vulgaris*

Buncle Hill (Buncle Edge)

There is a ridge of land now known as Buncle Edge that runs at about 250m between Stoneshiel Hill above the Whiteadder Water to the west and Warlawbank to the east that is crossed by the road between Preston and Grantshouse at Preston Cleugh. This ridge was predominantly moorland and rough grassland in Henderson's day (but is no longer so) and here he loved to walk, though it was at some distance from any of his homes. He records the scene around 1850 as follows (the botanical names are again updated):

'We now proceed on our ramble along Buncle Hill. We are at the Dog buss, a few stunted larch trees, above Crossgate Hall. From this spot there is a glorious prospect of the surrounding country. Several spots along the hill have been recently planted and all the young wood seems in thriving condition. Near the head of Fosterland burn, a celebrated fairy stream, we found several patches of the pleasant moorland plant Marsh Asphodel *Narthecium ossifragum*, several species of the Orchis tribe, Water Blinks *Montia fontana*, Creeping Cinquefoil *Potentilla reptans* and Tormentil *Potentilla erecta*.

On the east bank of Fosterland burn on the farm of Blackhouse another old British encampment may still be traced, but its trenches and area have been long under tillage. The Blaeberry and several fine ferns flourish abundantly on the banks of this stream. On the moor above Mayfield, the Moonwort *Botrychium lunaria* grows abundantly. This station for this rather rare fern was first pointed out by Mr R Dunlop. The same gentleman found in a bog near Mayfield the [sedge] *Carex viridula*.

Warlawbank is the name of an alpine farm near the eastern extremity of Buncle Hill. The farm house and onstead are situated a few paces to the south of another encampment which is in a pretty entire state. On the edges of this ancient fortification we found the Mountain Pansy *Viola lutea* in great abundance, with the Heath Bedstraw

Galium saxatile, Milkwort *Polygala serpyllifolia* and Heath Pea or Lickery Knots [Bitter-vetch] *Lathyrus linifolius*. The Dog Violet *Viola riviniana* and Wild Pansy *Viola tricolor* also grow in these trenches.

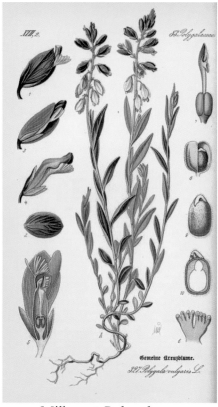

Milkwort *Polygala sp.*

It may be observed that, to a person taking a survey of these encampments on a fine summer day in July, few pleasanter views can be enjoyed. On the one hand are the wide heathy hills of Lammermoor, on the other the fertile vale of the Tweed, under the highest state of cultivation; its fields enclosed by well dressed thorn hedges, intermixed with belts and groves of trees sheltering the fields and ornamenting the seats of the gentry and the numerous neat and substantial farm steadings scattered everywhere about, its fields at that season of the year clothed with luxuriant crops of corn, verdant turnip plots, blooming potatoes or rich pastures with flocks and herds feeding or reposing in them with the clean silvery streams of the Tweed, Whitadder and lesser rivulets glancing in the sunbeams & meandering through the whole of the country bounded by the Cheviot mountains on the south, the hills of Teviotdale on the southwest, the Lammermoor hills on the north, and the ocean on the east, form altogether a landscape similar to a vast extended garden and which for beauty and fertility can scarcely be equalled in any quarter of the British Islands'.

It is reassuring that Henderson had learned to see value in the agricultural improvements and could still love his native countryside, despite his deep-felt belief that much had been lost unnecessarily: that a little thought to what we would today call wildlife conservation would have made a huge difference. He wrote: 'Our marshes and ponds might have suffered curtailment but surely there was no need that *every* piece of water and *every* bog and morass should have been destroyed'. His description confirms that by 1850 the transformation of the countryside was essentially complete with smallholdings and run-rig cultivation replaced by ordered fields and farmsteads.

Nature's Charms, published 1840

'Tis sweet to lie by mossy well,
Beside the blooming asphodel[1],
Or search the heath that skirts the dell
    For berries blae[2],
Where the green foxtail[3] decks the fell
    With lichens grey.

---

[1] Yellow Asphodel *Narthecium ossifragum*
[2] Blaeberry *Vaccinium myrtillus*
[3] Stag's-horn Clubmoss *Lycopodium clavatum*

Stag's-horn Clubmoss *Lycopodium clavatum*

There are still one or two such places in Berwickshire today, but not many, and one really has to travel north or west to experience moorland that is not intensively managed for grouse or planted with conifers.

The Fairies o' Fosterland[1], June 1855

This half-stanza, as quoted in Henderson's *Historical and Descriptive Account of Bunkle and Preston*, differs from the version published by Bill Henderson, which lacks the Moonwort.

> At midnight still on Mayfield hill,
> Where Moonwort[2] grew in dern[1],

---

[1] An old Berwickshire rhyme connects fairies with Fosterland: the Fosterland Burn runs south from the eastern end of Bunkle Edge above Blackhouse, and has an ancient encampment that was very strongly fortified by deep trenches and mounds of earth and stones, but was later 'demolished by the plough', though traces remain

[2] Moonwort *Botrychium lunaria*, along with Adder's-tongue Fern *Ophioglossum vulgatum*, was considered to be strongly associated with fairies

The fairy queen tript o'er the green,
'Mang heather-bells and fern.

Adder's-tongue Fern *Ophioglossum vulgatum*
and Moonwort *Botrychium lunaria*

There seems to be a deep-seated need within us to indulge in a little whimsy, or wizards would not remain so popular a subject. Sadly we must now use a TV or computer screen to aid our fancies as romantic places are just not there to be found in so much of our countryside.

---

[1] hiding

Chirnside and the Whiteadder Water

Most of the natural woodland in the Chirnside area, as in the Scottish Borders as a whole, had been lost long before Henderson's time in the centuries of border warfare. Many of the fragments that remained were along the riversides. There the wealthy landowners built their mansion houses and the woodlands were restored to some extent as a feature of their policies. Much Sycamore was introduced at this time along with Scots Pine, European Larch and Norway Spruce while other conifers from the New World were added later as they became available.

Whiteadder Water at Edrington

Chirnside was to be Henderson's home all his professional and married life. He was fond of walking by the Whiteadder below the village. Here are a few snippets to give an inkling of his life there.

One of Henderson's interests was the local proverbs of Berwickshire. Of the saying *'In the howe hole o' the Merse a' the folk are bannock-fed'* Henderson writes: 'The men of the Merse, have reason to be thankful for this distinction. The saying points to a period when barley instead of wheat was the staple grain of that fertile district; and my father remembers the time, when a cadger went once-a-week from Chirnside to Berwick for eighteenpence worth of wheaten bread, and he had often much difficulty in disposing of that quantity, which served the village and neighbourhood for a whole week; nobody then, about sixty years since, eating wheaten bread except infants and sick people. Pease-and-barley bannocks were then the staff of life; these are now scarcely ever seen, except in the houses of the hinds and cottars'.

Of Chirnside he writes: 'The houses in the village are interspersed with groups and single trees of venerable ash, elm and umbrageous sycamores which give the village a very picturesque appearance and make it very remarkable at a great distance'.

Of the rich farmland known as 'The Yolk of the Merse' he writes 'In the fields about Lintlaw we have observed a greater abundance of Corn Bluebottle or Blawort [Cornflower] *Centaurea cyanus* than we have seen anywhere else in the neighbourhood'. [Not far away, near Edrom, there is one field where this colourful weed still survives 150 years later].

As might be expected the Berwickshire Naturalists visited Chirnside. Here is the report of the meeting: 'The next meeting of the Club was at Chirnside, May 1st 1839 — as beautiful a morning as ever ushered in that month. The number of members present, notwithstanding the loveliness of the morning and the beauty of the spot selected for the meeting, were only Mr Selby, Rev T Riddell, Dr Johnston, Dr Clark, and Dr F Douglas. The party were afterwards joined by the Rev Mr Wilson, and Mr Henderson, surgeon, and felt much indebted to the latter gentleman for conducting them to the most favourable ground for observation. Their course was along the romantic wooded banks of the Whiteadder, where all the early spring flowers were in profuse blossom. Insects were tolerably abundant, and Mr Selby was successful in capturing several rather rare species. Several Flatworms *Planaria*, and ova, or spawn, of various fishes and insects, were procured from beneath the stones in the shallow channel of the river. Hairy Violet *Viola hirta* was found in full and luxuriant blossom, thereby adding another to the already numerous localities of this species in Berwickshire; which had been considered by Sir W Hooker as of very rare occurrence in Scotland. Tuberous Comfrey *Symphytum tuberosum* was likewise observed in considerable quantity, but not in flower. A rather singular twist, resembling in shape the top of a saddle, was observed in the limestone rock about a mile above Ninewells House, on the east side of the river. Beneath a projecting slab of this rock, a considerable quantity of acicular crystals of saltpetre was collected'.

Cornflower *Centaurea cyanus*

Whiteadder Water at Hutton Mill

Henderson jots down notes of a ramble by the Whiteadder at Blanerne on 5th May as follows: 'Beautiful haugh opposite the house, covered with roses, willows, alders &c. There will be found abundance of Butterbur *Petastites hybridus*, Marsh Marigold *Caltha palustris*, Lesser Marshwort *Apium inundatum*, Yellow Iris *Iris pseudacorus*, Great Willowherb *Epilobium hirsutum*, Mint, Horse Mint [*Mentha*], [Sedges] *Carices*. A little below the fine old ruin of the Border fortalice under the bank found a large patch of Lords-and-Ladies *Arum maculatum*. Above the house there is a splendid rookery and the bank for about a mile is clothed with the St John's-worts *Hypericum hirsutum*, *H. pulcrum* &c, Dog's Mercury *Mercurialis perennis* and the sweet Primrose *Primula vulgaris* in profuse and perfect beauty. On the steep bank a considerable distance above the old house found several specimens of the Wild Liquorice *Astragalus glycyphyllos* [now known at only two sites in the Scottish Borders], the Crane's-bills *Geranium pratense*, *G. robertianum* &c. On the haugh nearly opposite this spot found some specimens of the Cowslip *Primula veris* of a crimson colour, like some sorts of Polyanthus [likely to have been a hybrid between a garden plant and primrose], Barren Strawberry *Potentilla sterilis*. The Sloe *Prunus spinosa*, Hawthorn *Crataegus monogyna* and the Gooseberry *Ribes uva-crispa*. A little below the ford which crosses over to Todheugh, on the north side of the river, found a thick patch of Meadow Saxifrage *Saxifraga granulata*, and a little below this abundance of Creeping Cinquefoil *Potentilla reptans*. On the bank above the house found specimens of Speckled Wood Butterfly *Pararge aegeria* [this butterfly was to become locally extinct by 1890, but was seen again in 2007 and by 2009 appeared to be well established in Pease Dean on the Berwickshire coast]'.

Such notes show Henderson gathering the material he would use as a poet. Without making a complete list of the plants he captures the feel of the place well. The species he records show quite a close match to those that feature in his poems. I made my first such list at the age of 5½, so it was easy for me to fall back into the habit when life gave me the opportunity twenty years later. When did you last make such a list? Isn't it a way of working up one's appreciation of 'the wild'?

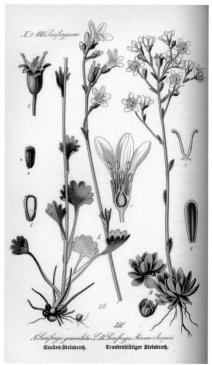

Meadow Saxifrage *Saxifraga granulata*

Nature's Charms, published 1840
Although a few birds do get a mention near the beginning, Henderson soon turns to botany, confirming his leanings.

> The hare-bell blue[1], in bushy glade,
> The violet[2] brooding in the shade,
> The cowslip's drooping cups inlaid
>   With spots of gold[3],
> Bring to my bosom thoughts arrayed
>   In magic's mould.

---

[1] Bluebell *Hyacinthoides non-scriptus* as proven by the woodland habitat in spring
[2] Common Dog-violet *Viola riviniana*
[3] Cowslip *Primula* veris has orange spots at the base of the petals

The globe-flower's[1] yellow nodding gem,
Richer than monarch's diadem,
The meadow's-queen[2] on taller stem,
    So scented sweet,
Bring back my early days with them,
      Whene'er we meet.

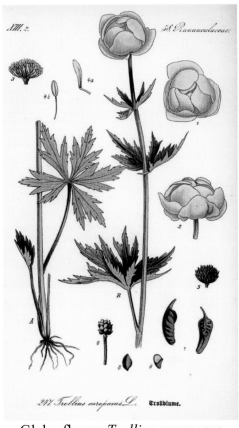

Globe-flower *Trollius europaeus*

---

[1] Globe-flower *Trollius europaeus* was known to Henderson by the Billie Burn
[2] Meadowsweet *Filipendula ulmaria*

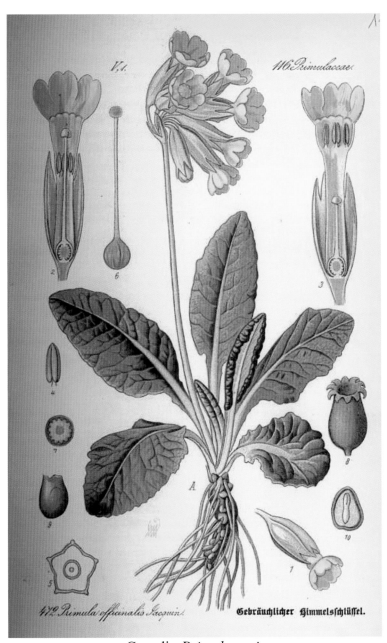

Cowslip *Primula veris*

Spring, published 1840
One line is unusual

The butter-burr hath burst in blossom from its urn.

Butterbur *Petastites hybridus* is one of the 'back-to-front plants', flowering before the leaves open, and its large flower-bud with greyish bracts is indeed very much like a funerary urn, once one has had one's eyes opened to the idea.

Butterbur *Petastites hybridus*

The Ever-Green Polypody, December 3, 1860
Botany does not have a close season in the winter after the flowers
have gone; there is always something to observe of trees or ferns.

> Along the muddy path, I trode but yesterday,
> From out a mossy wall[1] in thousand fronds of green
> The Polypody sprung, hanging each graceful spray,
> Over the crusted stones, and crevices between;

Polypody *Polypodium vulgare*

---

[1] Henderson gives the locality of the wall as between Hammerhall and the Piper's-
house, Blanerne. Polypody *Polypodium vulgare* still grows on this wall, just as he
describes

Spring has come, April 23, 1858
A familiar theme, which Henderson embraces with a freshness born
of close observation.

> The yellow coltsfoot o'er the lea,
>> In golden bloom comes forth
> While merry lapwings bounding flee
>> Cold winters to the north –

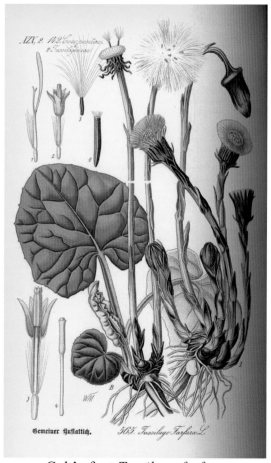

Colt's-foot *Tussilago farfara*

The Spring has come! with dewy feet
    She's passed the woodland glade,
And waked the fragile wind-flower[1] sweet,
    And gem'd each grassy blade.
The wood-sorrel[2] too appears again,
Pure, pale and white with purple vein,
    Drooping on mossy seat.

Wood Anemone *Anemone nemorosa*

---

[1] Wood Anemone *Anemone nemorosa*
[2] Wood Sorrel *Oxalis acetosella* is the emblem of the Berwickshire Naturalists' Club

Wood Sorrel *Oxalis acetosella*

An Autumn Ode, October 2, 1858

The trees selected are characteristic of the Borders, with oak omitted as it is not prominent around Chirnside. It is debateable just where the gean, Wild Cherry, is native, as it was and is much planted, but it comes away from suckers if felled and, with Wych Elm, is very characteristic of the scaurs by the Whiteadder which Henderson knew so well. The leaves of the ash are the last to open in spring and the first to fall in autumn.

> The gean-tree's foliage, crimson dyed,
> Glows beauteous on the forest side,
>   The elms grow yellow too;
> The ash's pale-green leaves drop down
> Upon the pathways damp and brown,
>   Which thickly they bestrew.

Solitude, December 28, 1859

A thoughtful poem: 'Tis not because I hate mankind, I seek the forest shade...

Where pale, the scented wood-riff[1] blooms upon the mossy brae,
And stately fox-glove's spotted bells, their lovely bloom display,
Where on the green untrodden bank, the cuckoo clover[2] springs,
And where the blue geranium[3] blows, and blithe the linnet sings.

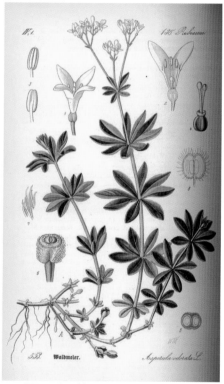

Woodruff *Galium odoratum*

---

[1] Woodruff *Galium odoratum*, a woodland plant
[2] Presumably an early-flowering clover, out in May when the cuckoo arrives, perhaps Lesser Trefoil *Trifolium dubium*
[3] Meadow Crane's-bill *Geranium pratense*

Our Hedge Side Flowers, September 1, 1860
Henderson weaves in as many plant names as he can without losing
the flow of his words.

> Blue-bells[1] bright, on slender stalk,
> Waving o'er the grassy balk;
> There the mill-foil's varied hues[2]
> In clustered beauty, bloom profuse,
> Mingled with the tall knop-weed[3],
> With its crown of lovely red,
> And the rest-harrow[4], creeping low,
> On the bank makes pleasant show,
> With the yellow agrimony[5],
> Smelling sweet, as new made honey.

---

[1] As this is late summer, Harebell *Campanula rotundifolia*
[2] Yarrow *Achillea millefolium* which is found in both white and pink-flowered forms
[3] Common Knapweed *Centaurea nigra*
[4] Common Restharrow *Ononis repens*
[5] Agrimony *Agrimonia eupatoria*, almost as scented as the locally rare Fragrant Agrimony *A. procera*

Knapweed *Centaurea sp.*

The Berwickshire Coast: St Abbs Head, Fast Castle and Dowlaw Dean

The Berwickshire coast from St Abbs Head to Fast Castle is marvellously rugged with towering cliffs and deep chasms and all naturalists find inspiration there. The geology is varied. St Abbs Head in particular is a 'seabird city' home to huge colonies of Guillemots with Razorbills, Fulmars and Kittiwakes that is now a National Nature Reserve. Its igneous rocks support a specialist flora as well as an abundance of familiar coastal species. Cliffs with dramatic folds of rock continue some miles west with a few remote beaches accessible with difficulty until Fast Castle Head is reached where there are romantic ruins. A little east of Fast Castle the line of the cliffs is broken by the deep chasm of Dowlaw Dean where an interesting flora contrasting with St Abbs Head greats the intrepid. The peregrine falcon is a feature of the coastline.

Henderson explored Fast Castle and nearby Dowlaw Dean in 1835, apparently with Alexander Carr, a fellow surgeon and fellow founder-member of the Berwickshire Naturalists' Club, as he refers to the locality in a poem to mark the death of Carr in 1839 at the tragically early age of 28, soon after he had joined the Navy as a surgeon. Carr published an account of the history and antiquities of Coldingham and adjoining parishes in 1836, and Henderson was inspired to do something similar for The Merse, so their friendship seems to have been a close one, founded on common interests.

View east from Ewelairs, by Pease Bay, to Fast Castle

Written in Dulaw Dean, near Fast Castle, in July, 1835

This glen is wild, and savage, lone, and deep.
    Its shattered rocks are all with lichen grey,
    And prickly brambles o'er their fragments stray;
The ivy green waves on the giddy steep,
And hawthorns hoar their nooks of shelter keep;
    The lowly rose-wort[1] decks the rugged brae,
The dark green alder o'er the brook does weep,
    And the tall willow-herb its rosy flowers display[2].

Roseroot *Sedum rosea*

Lines to the memory of Alexander Allan Carr, surgeon, Ayton, 1840

Only these lines survive, with a passing mention of Dowlaw Dean, as a footnote in Muirhead's *The Birds of Berwickshire*.

No more in Dowlaw's rugged dean we'll seek the rose-wort's flower,
Nor sit beside the murmuring brook at noon-tide's hour.

---

[1] Roseroot *Sedum rosea*: the most notable plant of the dean
[2] Rosebay Willowherb *Chamerion angustifolium*: a scarce plant then, but not so today

Fast Castle, July 5, 1856

This poem is set in May or early June, so seems not to relate to Henderson's July 1835 visit.

> Wild, on the ledge of ocean wide,
> > Thy ruins there remain;
> And the rude rocks laved by the tide,
> > Or wash'd by wintery rain,
> Still in their rugged forms abide
> > Whilst thou away dost wane.
> On the green downs that skirt the shore,
> > Blooms sweet the blue hare-bell[1],
> And mountain violets[2] spread their store
> > Fair by yon rocky dell[3].

Fast Castle

---

[1] Bluebell *Hyacinthoides non-scriptus* which grows here in plenty on the sea braes: Henderson would have enjoyed it as it is extraordinarily scarce around Chirnside. The two names Bluebell and Harebell are inextricably mixed, not least in the Borders where Scottish and English traditions mingle, but it matters little to the countryman as the flowering times are distinct. Henderson's Hare-bell follows Hooker's *Flora Scotica* 1821

[2] Mountain Pansy *Viola lutea*. I have searched for these in vain but they were refound by a visitor to the area in 2011

[3] Dowlaw Dean

Bluebell *Hyacinthoides non-scriptus*

A further stanza at the coast is given by Muirhead to illustrate his account of The Grey Sheeper or Rock Pipit.

> Down to the sea – where plashing laves
> The long sea-tangle amidst the waves;
> Over yon bank where the wood-vetch[1] clings
> In lovely bloom, and the Pipit sings.

---

[1] Wood Vetch *Vicia sylvatica* is one of the glories of the Berwickshire coast, found almost all the way north from Berwick to Linkim Shore and, north again, in and near Dowlaw Dean

St. Abbs, 23 November, 1859
A rugged headland, then as now a Mecca for all naturalists.

> Till all these rocks shall melt in fire,
> And nature in the flames expire;
> But till that morn of terror rise,
> Here shall be heard the sea-fowls' cries;
> Here on the rocks the flowers shall bloom,
> Here still shall wave the thistle's[1] plume,
> And wild-bees pass from flower to flower[2],
> And wild moors glisten in the shower,
> Of summer's sweet refreshing rain,
> And head-land stern, and level plain,
> And cove, and dell, and placid lake[3],
> To nature's votary still will make
> Sweet pictures to allure his eye,
> And cheer his heart 'neath cloud and sky.

Earnsheugh from St Abbs Head

---

[1] Could this be a reference to Slender Thistle *Carduus tenuifolius*, something of a speciality of the Head?
[2] The bumblebees have a particular liking for Purple Milk-vetch *Astragalus danicus*, which flourishes there
[3] This must be Coldingham Loch as the dam which created Mire Loch was not built until 1900

The Lammermuirs

While Henderson could find moorland at Bunkle Edge quite close to his home, he knew Dirrington Law beyond Duns and ventured on occasion up the Whiteadder Water to the hills around Abbey St Bathans. He also reached the upper Whiteadder above Cranshaws, with a strong suggestion in his poems of at least one occasion when, as a student in Edinburgh, he found a lift to Gifford and walked home over the Lammermuirs possibly taking in Meikle Says Law before dropping down to the Killpalet Burn, the Faseny Water and the Whiteadder Water where the Whiteadder Reservoir now lies.

The Lammermuirs have changed much in recent years with an electricity power line, well-engineered access tracks and now with large wind farms. There is still much heather but it is all burnt to a rotation with military precision that often fails to leave sanctuaries up remote burnsides. Despite this, much of the grandeur remains and botanical gems are still hidden away including populations of Hairy Stonecrop *Sedum villosum*, though this species may not have been known to Henderson.

Heather *Calluna vulgaris*

Moorland Joy, April 19, 1856

No trace of sorrow here: the Lammermuirs were still sufficiently pristine to 'make the lone heart gladly beat'. Botanists in the hills gravitate naturally to springs or 'flushes' with their diverse plant communities dominated by sedges searching for special favourites such as Grass-of-Parnassus *Parnassia palustris*.

Grass-of-Parnassus *Parnassia palustris*

Did you sit beside the fountain[1],
Far away among the heather?
Did you listen to its murmurs,
While its mosses green you'd gather?
Did you hear the gentle breezes
Moaning through the hair-grass tall[2]?
And mark the mist wreaths on the mountain
When the day was near the fall?

View from Hule Moss to the Dirringtons

The Rush-Bush, October 7, 1859

The botanist is rather dismissive of the Common Rush *Juncus effusus*, as it is often found where there has been partial drainage and where it displaces Jointed Rush *Juncus articulatus* and many other plant species. Henderson rises above this prejudice.

I love the Rush that greenly grows
Where fount or rill serenely flows;
I love the Rush that bending low
Upon the pool its shade doth throw;

---

[1] spring
[2] Tufted Hair-grass *Deschampsia cespitosa*

On marshy spot, or mossy stank,
The Rush-bush, rising strong and rank,
    I love to view when leaves are sear,
And when, through withered hair grass long,
The autumn-winds, a solemn song
    Pour forth unto the waning year.

Common Rush *Juncus effusus*

Up to the Moors, April 7, 1860

A happy poem that winds its way up the Whiteadder visiting the choice scenic spots in turn.

I love to see the purple bloom across the moorlands spread,
The heather-blooms o' Lammermoor, I love, I love, to tread;
I love to wander by the marsh that plough has never torn,
I love to see the rush-tufts wave where ne'er has wav'd the corn.

The yellow club moss[1] creeping low by mound and mossy stone,
The blae-berry[2] on the sunny brae, are sweet to look upon;
Far on the dark deep well below is pictured *Ordweil* steep,
And through the *Strait-loup*'s pass above the roaring waters leap.

---

[1] Stag's-horn Clubmoss *Lycopodium clavatum*
[2] *Vaccinium myrtillus*, never Bilberry in Scotland

Dr George Johnston and
The Berwickshire Naturalists' Club

As mentioned earlier, Henderson was a founder member of the Berwickshire Naturalists' Club. The Club's founder, Dr George Johnston of Berwick-upon-Tweed, was a remarkable man with success not only in his medical practice and in his natural history, for which he gained recognition throughout Britain, but also in local politics, serving three terms as mayor of Berwick.

On the death of Dr George Johnston of Berwick-upon-Tweed,
August 1, 1855
Of this fine memorial to the Club's founder I give just two stanzas:

> Yet he his day hath spent right well,
> And left precious works to tell
> Of beauties that in Nature dwell; –
> Those books will bide,
> And bear his name with gentle spell,
> Down Time's far tide.
>
> May wild flowers deck thy verdant grave,
> Red thyme, and bluebells o'er thee wave,
> And heaven's soft dews for ever lave
> Thy place of rest!
> For thee, lover of Nature! Now we crave
> Peace in her breast!

Wild Thyme *Thymus polytrichus*

Johnston writes in *The Natural History of the Eastern Borders* 'An anonymous contributor to Hone's *Every Day Book*, vol. i. p.901, has so graphically described the stations of our *Campanula* – his Bellflower – that I cannot resist the temptation of quoting some of the stanzas' [the stanzas he chose are those reproduced here but with stanza four omitted]. Johnston quotes from several of Henderson's poems in his book so it seems he had no reason to attribute this poem to Henderson, as I was at first inclined to. Henderson's style developed over the years and the date is rather early for so polished a poem and some touches are not quite in his usual character. But there is a more telling reason for doubt: it relates to the glow worm. Henderson only wrote about natural history that he had observed himself and we happen to know that he did not have his first encounter with a glow worm until 1843 as he wrote it up for the Berwickshire Naturalists' Club's journal, or *History*, while the poem was published in 1825. So the poem is not his. Nevertheless both the glow worm story and the poem are such good examples of the wide interests of the Berwickshire Naturalists' Club that I reproduce them both here.

Henderson writes: 'On passing up the post-road [now the A1], on the evening of the 5th of August last [1843], between Houndwood Inn and Renton, I observed 'a modest ray' emanating from the wooded bank on the north side of the road. I was convinced that it was the lamp of the glow-worm, although I had never before seen it; but being then on a professional visit, I had no time to stop, and examine from what source the light proceeded. It was one of the mildest and most beautiful nights of the season, and, on my return, about midnight, I fondly expected again to see the object of my wishes. I was not disappointed; at the same spot, the insect was diffusing its mild radiance on the grass and bushes in its vicinity. The light appeared most beautiful, and I could not help exclaiming with the poet, surely

> There's not a fairer beam than this
> In all the expanse of day!

I alighted and captured the creature from the top of a long stalk of grass, on which it had taken up its station'.

Seeking to learn more about glow worms I contacted Robin Scagell of the UK Glow Worm Survey who replied 'Last summer [2009] I received a very interesting report from a railway worker of glow worms seen on the main East Coast railway line near Penmanshiel [just a couple of miles from Henderson's locality]. There is a long-standing question about why glow worms are so often found along railway lines. Your report of glow worms that existed long before the railway (and indeed the modern road-building system) suggest that in this location at least, there was a historic population of glow worms that has been preserved along the railway line'.

As to the poem, it runs:

To the Bellflower[1]

With drooping bells of clearest blue
Thou didst attract my childish view,
   Almost resembling
The azure butterflies[2] that flew
Where on the heath thy blossoms grew
   So lightly trembling.

Where feathery fern and golden broom
Increase the sandrock[3] cavern's gloom
   I've seen thee tangled,
'Mid tufts of purple heather bloom
By vain Arachne's treacherous loom[4]
   With dewdrops spangled.

'Mid ruins tumbling to decay,
Thy flowers their heavenly hues display,
   Still freshly springing,
Where pride and pomp have passed away
On mossy tomb and turret gray,
   Like friendship clinging.

When glowworm lamps illume the scene
And silvery daisies dot the green,
   Thy flowers revealing,
Perchance to soothe the fairy queen,
With faint sweet tones on night serene,
   Soft bells are pealing.

---

[1] Harebell *Campanula rotundifolia* for which Round-leaved Bellflower was given
as an alternative name in Hooker's *Flora Scotica* 1821
[2] Common Blue butterfly
[3] sandstone rock
[4] spider's web

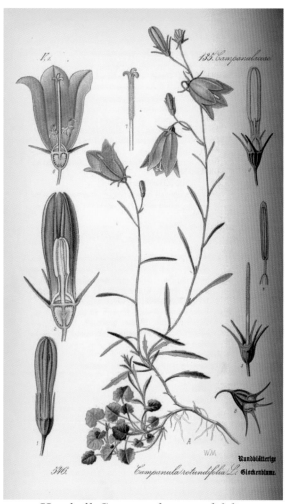

Harebell *Campanula rotundifolia*

But most I love thine azure braid,
When softer flowers are all decayed,
   And thou appearest
Stealing beneath the hedgerow shade,

Like joys that linger as they fade,
   Whose last are dearest.

Thou art the flower of memory;
The pensive soul recalls in thee
   The year's past pleasures;
And, led by kindred thought, will flee,
Till, back to careless infancy,
   The path she measures.

Billie Castle (ruins)

Acknowledgements

The author thanks Bill Henderson for his generosity in permitting such extensive extracts from his book *Merse Local Rhymes and Other Poems* and Carol Jefferson-Davies for reading his early drafts and persuading him to record his own perceptions of the countryside.

Extracts from *Berwickshire Mss* are published with the kind permission of Scottish Borders Archive & Local History Centre.

The plates from O W Thomé's *Flora von Deutschland Österreich und der Schweiz* are available on the internet at http://caliban.mpiz-koeln.mpg.de/thome/index.html. The illustration of oxen ploughing is reproduced courtesy of the Science Museum, London.

References

Carr, A A, 1836, *The History of Coldingham Priory*, A & C Black, Edinburgh and Longman, London.

Hardy, J, 1900, *The Session Book of Bunkle and Preston*, with, Ferguson, J, ed., *Historical and Descriptive Account of Bunkle and Preston*, The Berwickshire Naturalists' Club, Berwick-upon-Tweed.

Henderson, G, c. 1851, *Berwickshire Mss*, Vols I-III, transcriptions of part of the notebooks of Dr George Henderson, SBA/265, Scottish Borders Archive & Local History Centre, Heritage Hub, Hawick.

Henderson, W G, 2009, *Merse Local Rhymes and other Poems*, Eskbank Books, Edinburgh.

Johnston, G, 1829, 1831, *A Flora of Berwick-upon-Tweed*, 2 Vols, J Carfrae and Son, Edinburgh and Longman, London.

Johnston, G, 1853, *The Natural History of the Eastern Borders*, J van Voorst, London.

Knight, Rev T, 1839, Presidential Address, in: *History of the Berwickshire Naturalists' Club*, I. 180.

Muirhead, G, 1889, 1895, *The Birds of Berwickshire*, 2 Vols, David Douglas, Edinburgh.

Parry, M L, Slater, T R, eds., 1980, *The Making of the Scottish Countryside*, Croom Helm, London.

The Berwickshire Naturalists' Club membership is around 300.

The main emphasis of the Club's activities is on antiquities and local history expressed by five field meetings a year between May and September to places of interest between the Forth and the Tyne where an expert usually gives a talk and helps to take members round. Such places include historic private houses not open to the public. In addition there are usually two extra meetings of a botanical or ornithological nature.

There are also two indoor meetings when talks are given. The President of the Club gives the 'Anniversary Address' at the Annual General Meeting in October and an 'Autumn Lecture', usually on a natural history topic, is given in November.

The Club publishes a journal once a year, the 'History', which includes papers on a wider range of subjects than the field meetings including archaeology, cultural history and natural history. The authors are mainly Club members and the papers are at a refreshingly varied level of expertise.

The Club has an extensive Library open to members in Berwick Museum and to *bona fide* researchers via the Berwick Record Office.

Contact details
Corresponding Secretary, Mrs Susanna Arnott, The Old Granary, New Mains, Foulden, Berwick-upon-Tweed TD15 1UL
Library, c/o Berwick Museum & Art Gallery, Ravensdowne Barracks, Berwick-upon-Tweed TD15 1DG

The Author

Michael Braithwaite lives near Hawick and since 1979 has been the Botanical Recorder for Berwickshire for the Botanical Society of the British Isles, of which he has recently completed a term as President. He is a regular contributor to the 'History' of The Berwickshire Naturalists' Club and to the journals of the Botanical Society of the British Isles (BSBI).